EASY-TO-MAKE STAINED GLASS BOXES

WITH FULL-SIZE TEMPLATES

ED SIBBETT, JR.

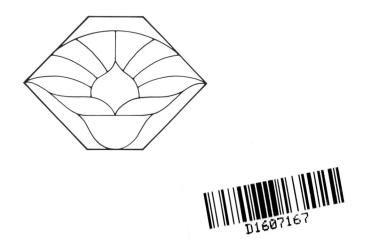

DOVER PUBLICATIONS, INC.

NEW YORK

Published in Canada by General Publishing Company, Ltd., 30 Lesmill Road, Don Mills, Toronto, Ontario.
Published in the United Kingdom by Constable and Company, Ltd.

Easy-to-Make Stained Glass Boxes: With Full-Size Templates is a new work, first published by Dover Publications, Inc., in 1984.

International Standard Book Number 0-486-24560-8

Manufactured in the United States of America
Dover Publications, Inc., 31 East 2nd Street, Mineola, N.Y. 11501

INTRODUCTION

Square, rectangular, circular, hexagonal or octagonal; crowned with a flat, rimmed, sloped or layered top; studded with glass jewels and mirror sections or left unembellished in their streaked and rippled splendor, stained glass boxes evince a delicate, self-contained beauty. One of the most popular of glassworking projects and one well suited for classes, constructing boxes is a natural direction for craftspeople to turn to when they have mastered two-dimensional copper foil panels and wish to venture into the third dimension. Glassmasters who have set their sights on putting together lampshades will find box-making a valuable learning experience and a rewarding challenge. The uses for stained glass boxes are almost unlimited—jewel boxes, centerpieces, cigar boxes, bookends—and they can be adapted, by eliminating tops and certain glass pieces, into terrariums, candle shelters, tissue boxes, letter holders or other containers.

This book contains full-size templates for constructing 42 different boxes featuring designs with floral, butterfly, heart, geometric, abstract, Art Nouveau and Art Deco motifs. The basic square or rectangular box includes six panels: a many-pieced top, four complementary sides and a one-piece bottom. The more complex patterns add more sides and offer many varieties of box tops. The simplest six-panel patterns require as few as 20 glass pieces while the more challenging patterns include up to 22 template sections and 133 glass pieces.

Instructions are given for assembling the panels and box and attaching hinges, but you should be familiar with the basic tools, materials and techniques of stained glass work before attempting these projects. Novice craftspeople may wish to consult an introductory manual such as *Stained Glass Craft* by J.A.F. Divine and G. Blachford (Dover Publications, 0-486-22812-6) or attempt some of the projects in Ed Sibbett, Jr.'s *Contemporary Stained Glass Projects* (Dover, 0-486-23559-9). These and other books on the craft will help you choose glass suitable for your project and instruct you in proper cutting and grozing techniques.

Materials

Besides the basic tools and materials needed for copper-foiling, you should have a wood block or similar object to prop up panels when you are soldering them together. Carpenter's squares are recommended for checking the boxes' corner angles. If you are planning to attach hinges to the box you will need a pair of small pliers to hold them while soldering. Felt pieces are helpful for cushioning the bottom of the box.

Antique, cathedral and opalescent glass, separately or in combination, are all suitable to be cut for the pieces of the templates. Round and diamond-shaped faceted glass jewels can be used to highlight a design, as shown on Pattern 16. The jewels can be replaced with other pieces if you prefer not to use faceted glass. Mirror glass, which comes in a variety of colors and thicknesses, is often used for the bottom panels, as on the square box on the front cover of the book.

How to Use the Templates

The 42 patterns in this book can be used to make one of the 11 types of boxes shown in Figure 1. The directions on the plates note the pattern pieces needed for constructing boxes and identify the type of box the patterns will make. Top templates are included for each pattern along with at least one of all the different sizes and designs of side and top side templates, which are usually repeated. The number in brackets in the list of parts in the plate directions indicates the number of times that a template should be repeated (combined totals are given for some cases, such as Patterns 39 and 40, where the same template design is shown more than once). The bottom template is sometimes the same size as the top, and is then marked "sst" in the plate directions, but usually it is made from one piece of glass instead of repeating the top design. For patterns with angled tops and tops with projections, dimensions are given in the directions for flat, straight-edged bottoms. (*Note:* all measurements given for templates in this book are only approximate. Adjustments will probably

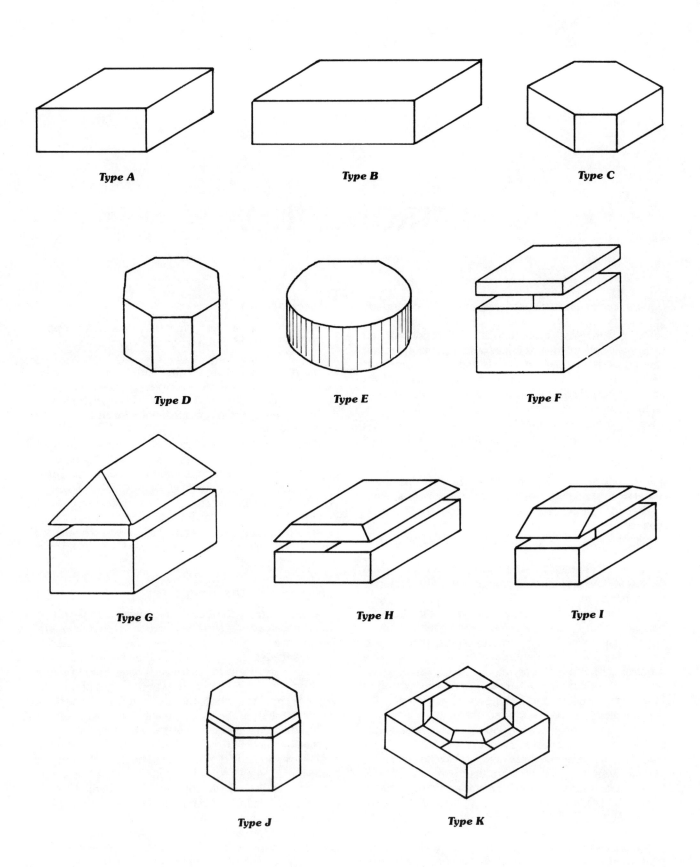

Type A

Type B

Type C

Type D

Type E

Type F

Type G

Type H

Type I

Type J

Type K

Figure 1

need to be made to compensate for small inaccuracies made while cutting out glass pieces.)

If you want to include hinges on the box, you should make one side (called the back) ⅛″ lower on top than the other sides. The gap at the top of the back will require minor adjustments to the design on the back template of Patterns 9, 31, 33 and 34. Which side you make the back is your option, but on rectangular and hexagonal boxes one of the side A panels is usually chosen.

It is important to keep the edges of the heavyweight paper as neat and firm as possible, so use very sharp scissors or an X-ACTO knife when cutting out a template (you may want to remove the entire page from the book). Trace the template onto a sheet of tracing paper before cutting the template into individual pieces. The tracing is then used as a reference when the time comes to assemble the pieces to form a box panel. Number the pieces on the template and on the tracing. Determine the number of panels and glass pieces the box will require and make a color rendering of the design showing the kind of glass used for each piece. The color renderings of the patterns on the covers offer design possibilities.

Copper Foil Technique

Begin by assembling the individual panels using the copper foil technique. Use adhesive-backed copper foil, which is available in 36-yard rolls, in widths of ³⁄₁₆″, ¼″, ⅜″ and ½″. After cutting the glass, clean off oil and wrap a thin strip of foil around the edges of each piece. Make certain that the glass is centered over the foil so that it extends an equal distance on both sides of the glass. The foil strip should be long enough to go around all the edges of the piece and overlap itself by about ¼″. Press the foil carefully and firmly into place using a fid, burnisher or pencil. Trim excess foil at the corners with a scissors, razor blade or X-ACTO knife.

Fit the glass pieces of an individual panel together, treating the top side and multi-part top template sections in Patterns 29–42 as separate units. Tack the corners of each piece of glass by holding a soldering iron over the corners and dropping a piece of solder onto the corner. Coat the foil with a thin layer of flux and then move the soldering iron along the foil while pulling the solder close behind. On contact with the foil, the solder should melt and spread out along the entire width of the foil. Repeat this procedure with the other panels that contain more than one piece of glass.

Assembling the Box

When building any three-dimensional project, care must always be taken to work at a proper angle for soldering. Make sure that the solder will not merely drip down onto your working surface, but rather will flow down into the seam being joined. Prop up panels with wooden blocks or other heavy objects as shown in Figure 2.

The important thing to keep in mind when making boxes is that at the intersection of panels a groove must remain on the outside of the box so that it can be soldered

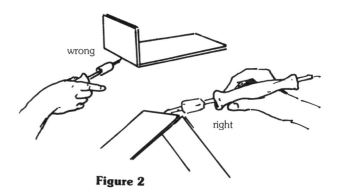

Figure 2

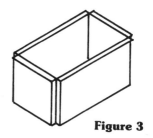

Figure 3

properly (see Figure 3). To assemble the body of the box, place one of the side pieces in position, perpendicular to the bottom panel. Run the soldering iron along the groove formed by the outside seam, or flux and add a drop of solder at the ends of the seam; this will tack the pieces together but allow them to be moved enough to make last-minute corrections. One by one, put the other sides in position and tack them together. When all sides are in proper alignment with the bottom and each other, flux each seam and coat with a heavy application of solder.

Boxes with square or rectangular bodies can be assembled by tacking the sides together first and then adding the bottom. Strips of masking tape placed around the inside and outside of the four sides (see Figure 4) will hold the side in position while you tack. Again, be sure that the inner edges meet to form the outside groove. After you have tacked the bottom in position, flux the seams and solder.

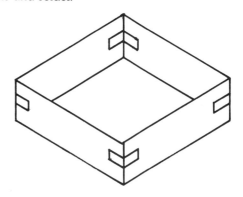

Figure 4

Three-dimensional box tops (Patterns 29–42) can be assembled in a similar manner, tacking the top sides one by one onto the top and each other. Some of the top sides are attached perpendicular to the top, others are splayed at an angle. For the box tops in Patterns 41 and 42, the inner tier of trapezoidal shaped pieces should be tacked to the octagonal panel and to each other splayed at a 135° angle. Each panel of the outer tier, which lies parallel to the top octagon, is then tacked to the pieces of the inner tier with the groove on the underside of the box top. When all adjacent pieces have been tacked and adjusted, the seams can be fluxed and soldered.

To avoid scratching furniture surfaces, glue felt pieces to the bottom of the box. If the bottom is of mirror glass, use special adhesive-backed felt instead. If you are attaching hinges to the box, wait until the operation is complete before gluing felt to the bottom.

Hinges

When the top and body of the box are assembled you may wish to join them together with hinges. Three types of hinges are described below. Not all boxes need to have hinges; loose tops can be slid or lifted off the box. Hinges can easily be subjected to too much strain and wrench free from the box, pulling the foil with them. Care should be taken to insure that the edges to which the hinges will be attached are sufficiently firm.

As mentioned before, the back panel to which you will be attaching the hinges should be ⅛" lower at the top than the other side panels. (Note: Patterns 11 and 15 have projections on one edge of the top; this is the front edge.) Strengthen the top edge of the back and back edge of the top with additional strips of foil. If you are using small brass flanged hinges, adding an extra wide strip of foil will give the flanges more edge to latch onto.

Flanged brass box hinges. The small, solid brass square hinges commonly found on wooden boxes can be obtained in crafts or glass supply stores. These hinges are best used with smaller boxes because they are vulnerable to stress. Usually two hinges are used, positioned near the corners (see Figure 5). Snip off any part of the flanges that protrudes onto the glass surface.

Flux and tin the hinge flanges, being careful not to let any drops fall into the hinge workings. Hold one of the hinges with a small pair of pliers—brass gets hot during soldering—and solder it to the foil edge on the back; repeat with the other hinge. Then hold the box top in position and solder the hinges to it. An extra-firm bond can be formed by gluing the hinge to the box with strong cement before soldering.

Spiral loop hinges. These hinges consist of two thick brass wires bent into two or three spiral loops into which is run brass wire that has been soldered to the edge of the box from bottom to top. After fluxing and tinning, the loops are soldered to the top along its back edge, a fraction or so from the corner. The wires for the side edges should be cut long enough for them to be attached along the entire height of the back panel with a part left over to be bent over and inserted through the loops connected to the top (see Figure 6). Flux, tin and solder the wires in the back side seams and then place the top in position and insert wires in loops.

Tube hinge. The tube hinge works on the same principle as the spiral loop hinge, but the loops are replaced by a brass tube that is soldered along the top's back edge (Figure 7), again with openings for wires a fraction or so from the corners.

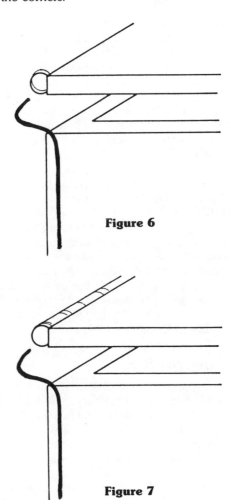

Figure 6

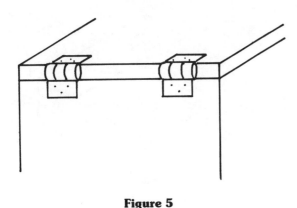

Figure 5

Figure 7

EASY-TO-MAKE STAINED GLASS BOXES

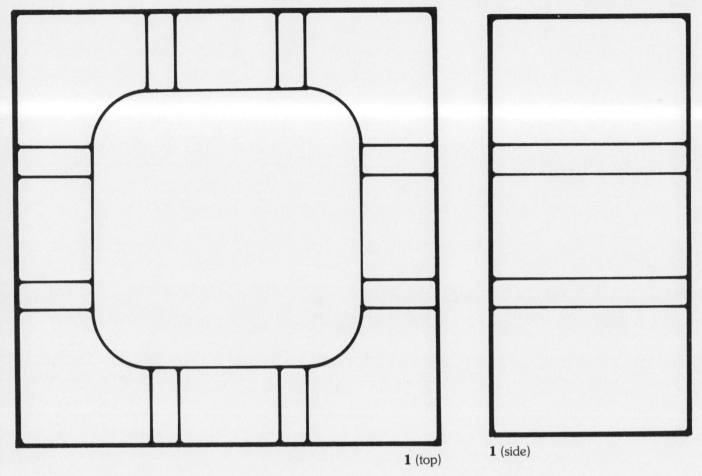

1 (top)

1 (side)

Patterns 1 and 2: top, side [4], bottom (sst). Type A

2 (side)   **2** (top)

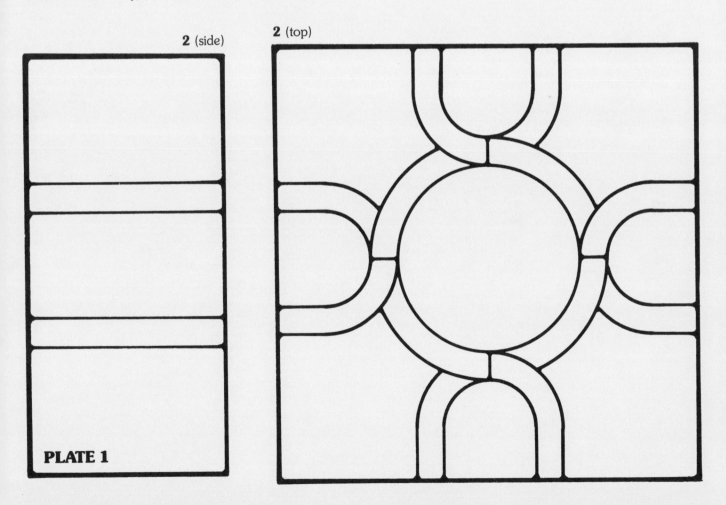

PLATE 1

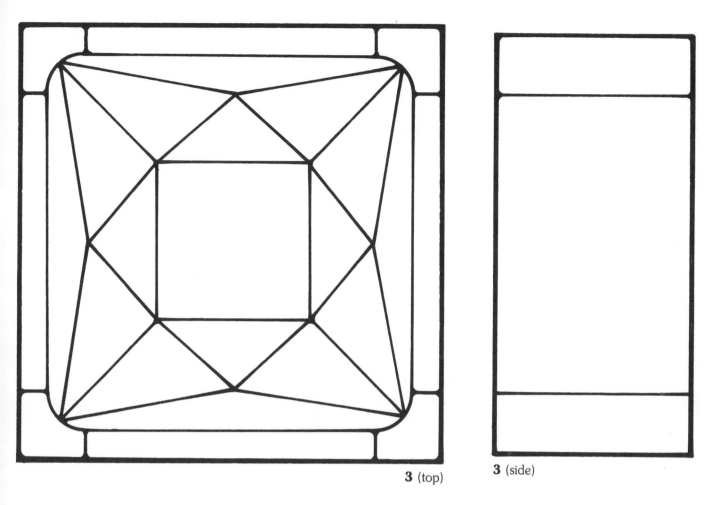

3 (top)   **3** (side)

Patterns 3 and 4: top, side [4], bottom (sst). Type A

4 (side)   **4** (top)

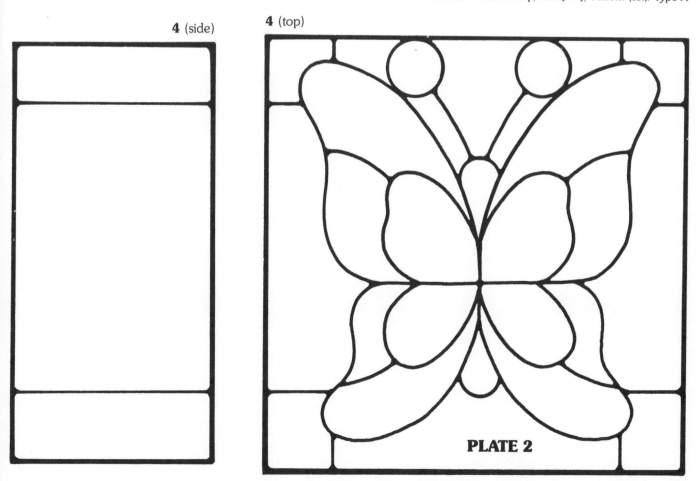

PLATE 2

5 (top)

5 (side)

Patterns 5 and 6: top, side [4], bottom (sst). Type A

6 (side)

6 (top)

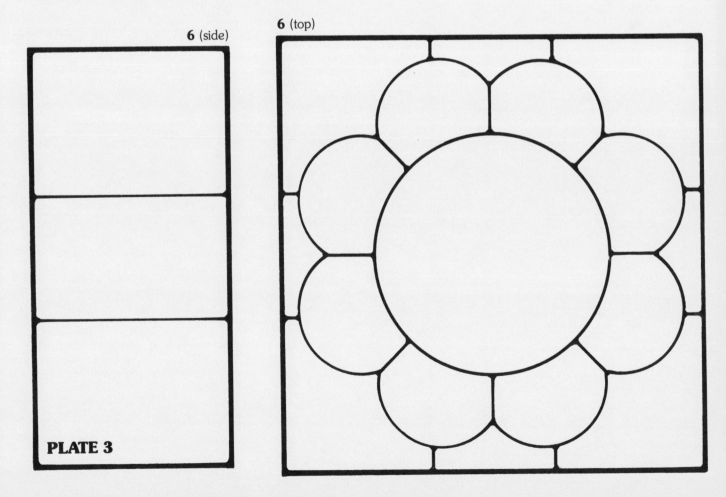

PLATE 3

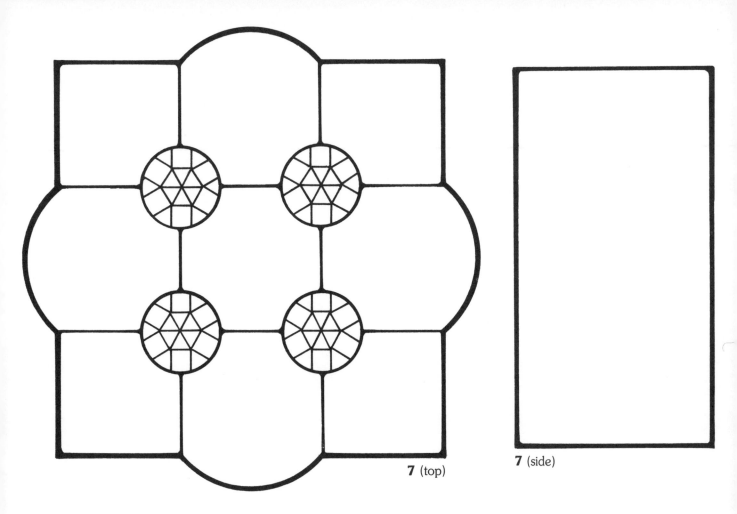

7 (top)

7 (side)

Patterns 7 and 8: top, side [4], bottom (Patt. 7: 4⅛″ square; Patt. 8: sst). Type A

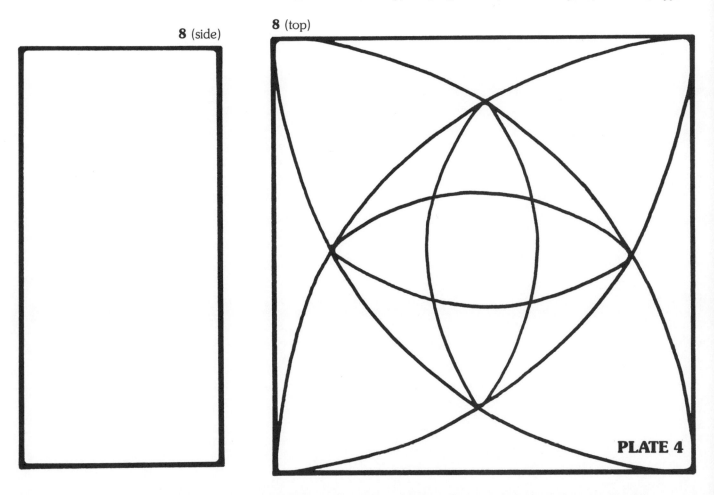

8 (side)

8 (top)

PLATE 4

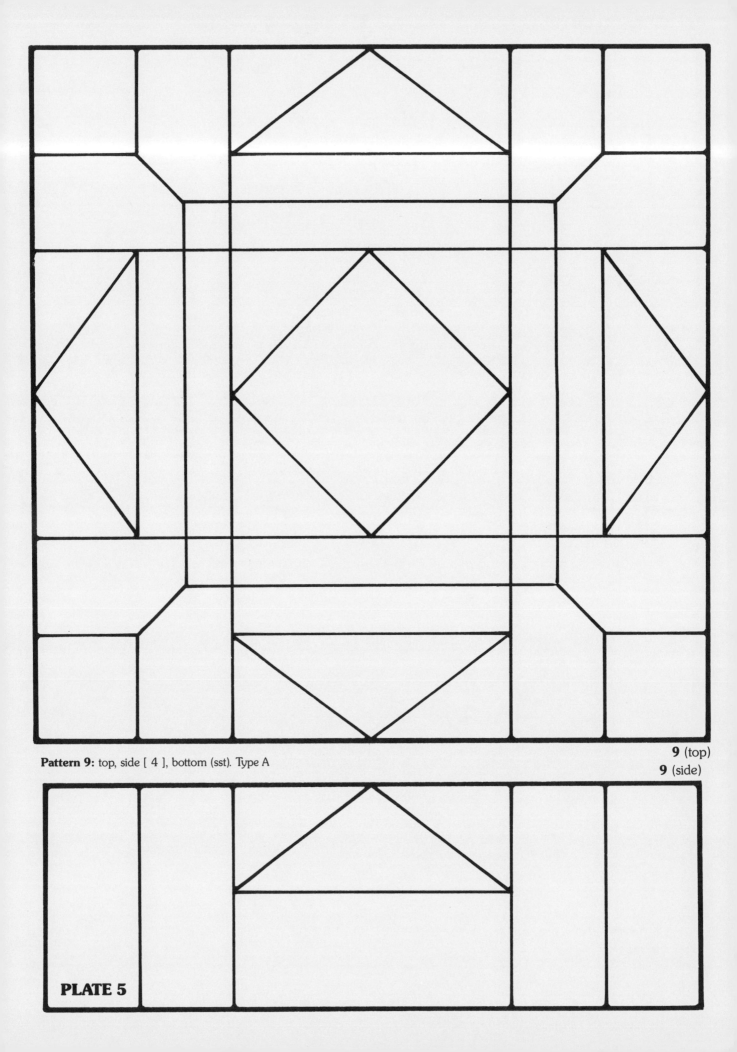

Pattern 9: top, side [4], bottom (sst). Type A

9 (top)
9 (side)

PLATE 5

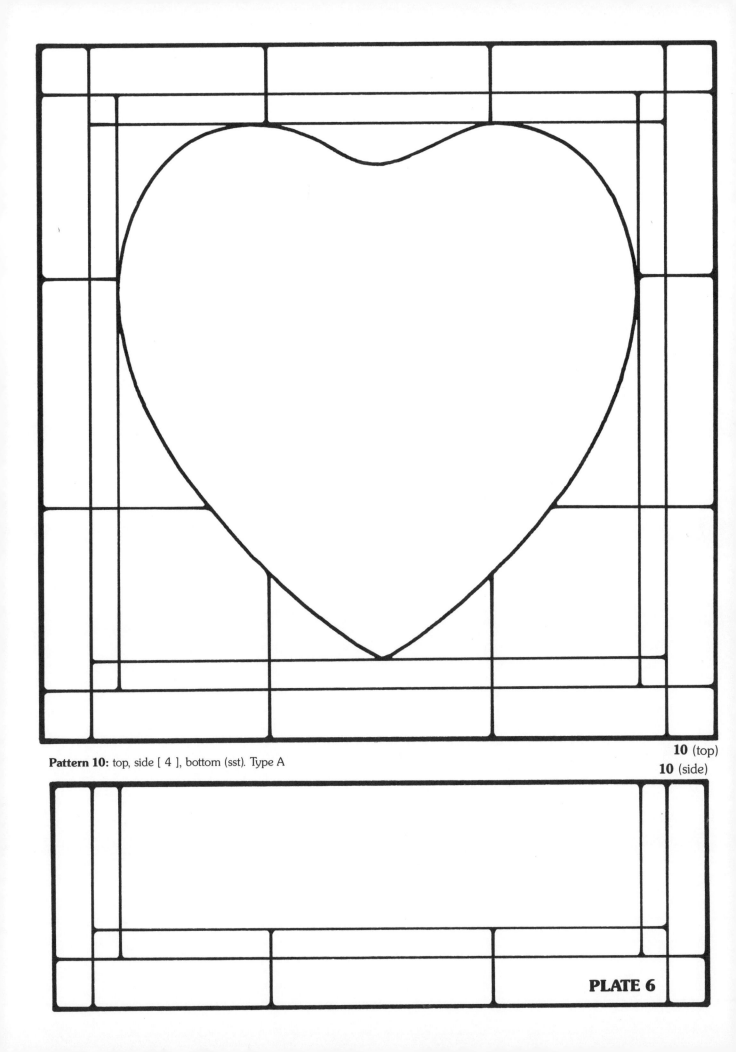

Pattern 10: top, side [4], bottom (sst). Type A

10 (top)
10 (side)

PLATE 6

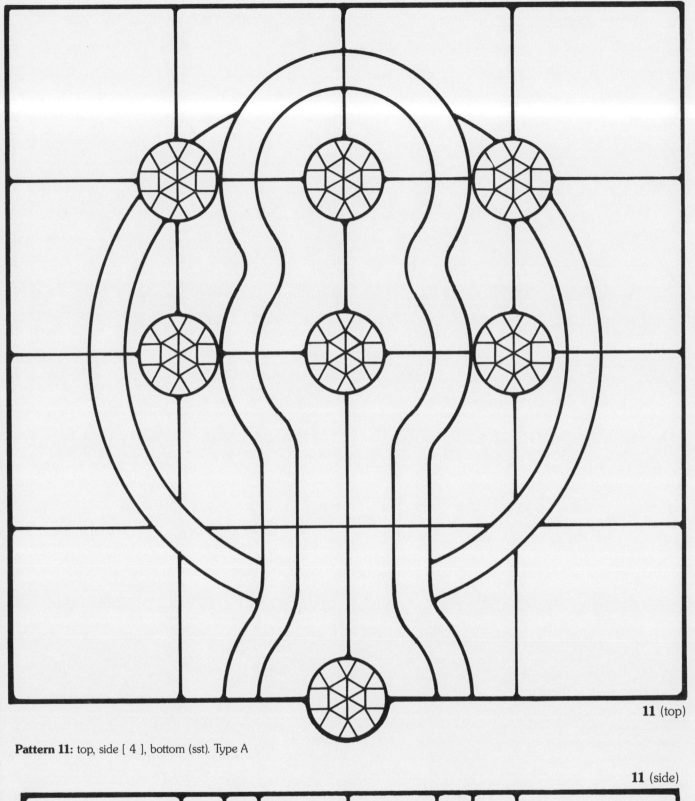

11 (top)

Pattern 11: top, side [4], bottom (sst). Type A

11 (side)

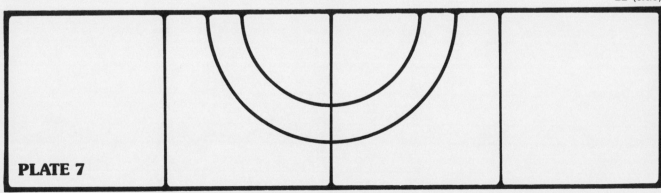

PLATE 7

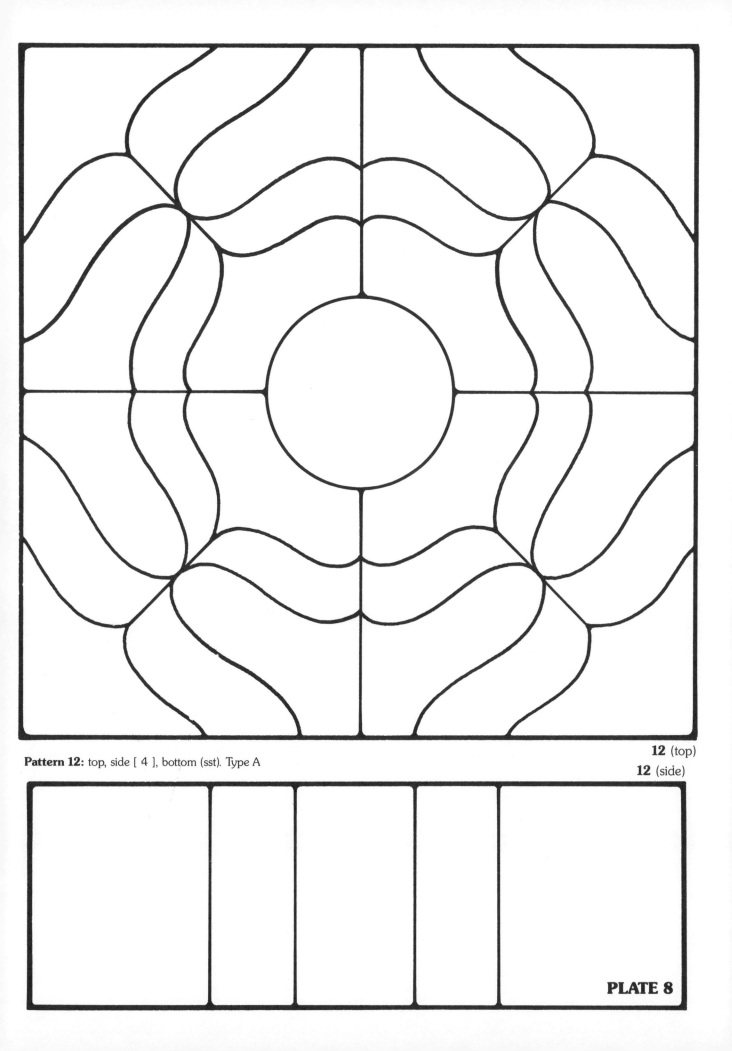

Pattern 12: top, side [4], bottom (sst). Type A

12 (top)

12 (side)

PLATE 8

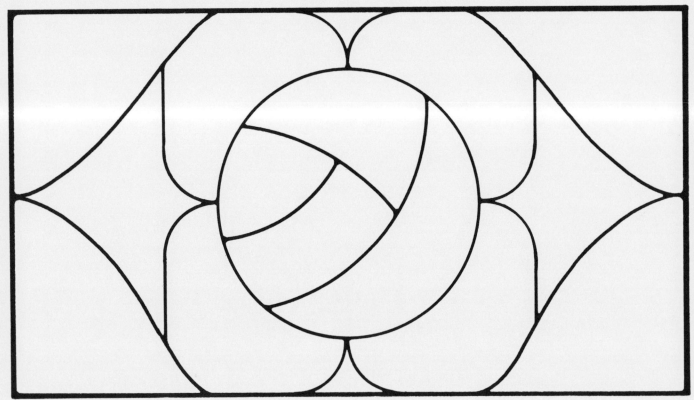

13 (top)

Patterns **13–15:** top, side A [2], side B [2], bottom (Patt. 13 and Patt. 14: sst; Patt. 15: 7¼ × 4). Type B

14 (top)

PLATE 9

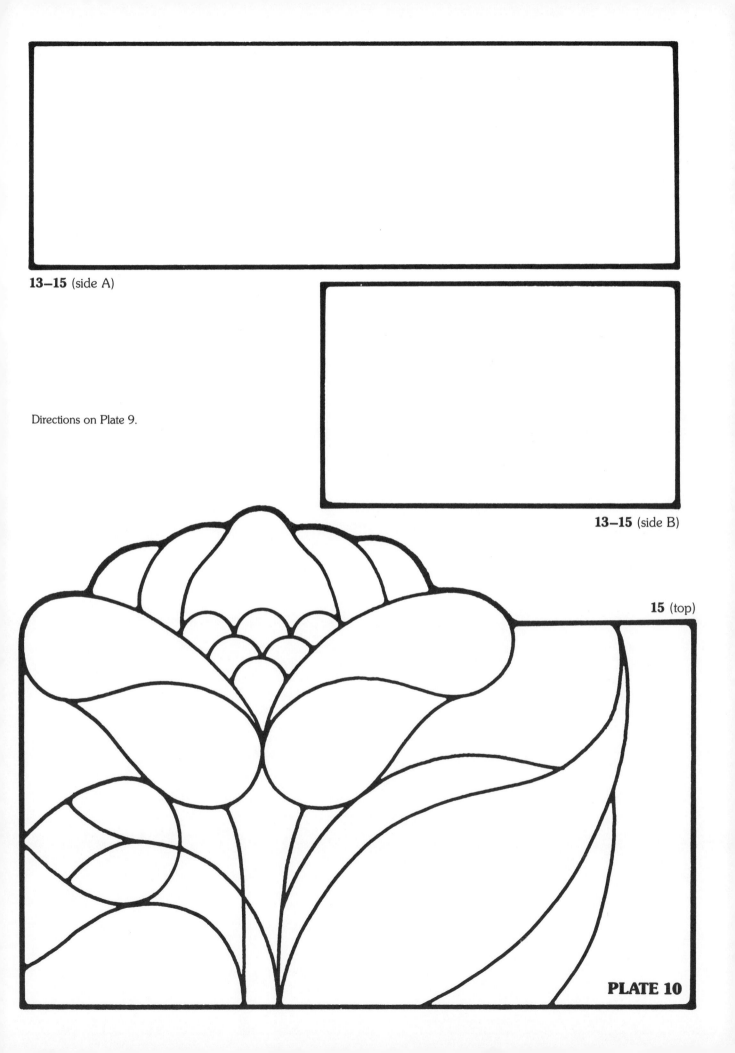

13–15 (side A)

Directions on Plate 9.

13–15 (side B)

15 (top)

PLATE 10

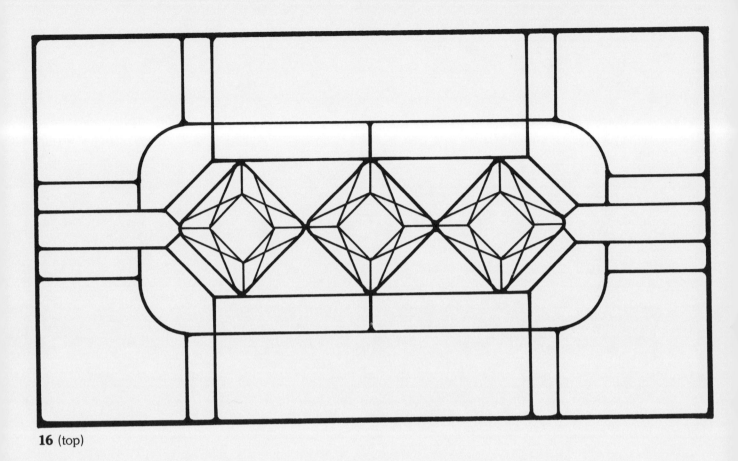

16 (top)

Patterns 16—18: top, side A [2], side B [2], bottom (sst). Type B

17 (top)

PLATE 11

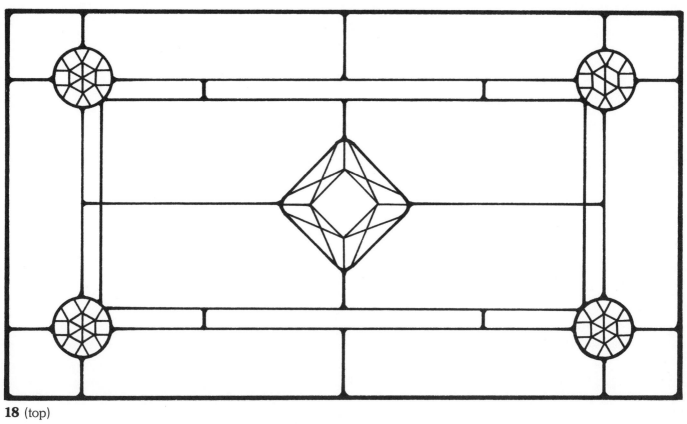

18 (top)

16–18 (side B)

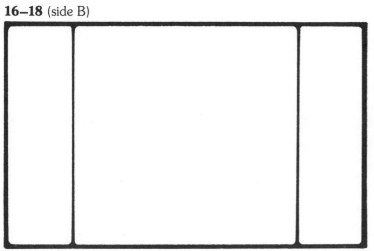

Directions on Plate 11.

16–18 (side A)

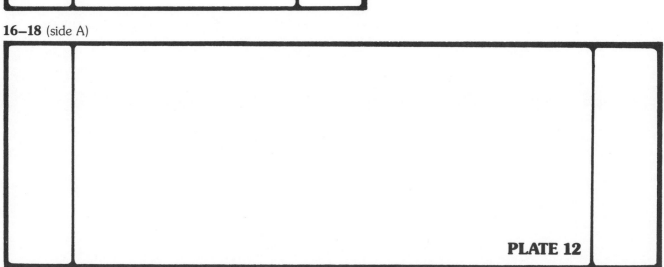

PLATE 12

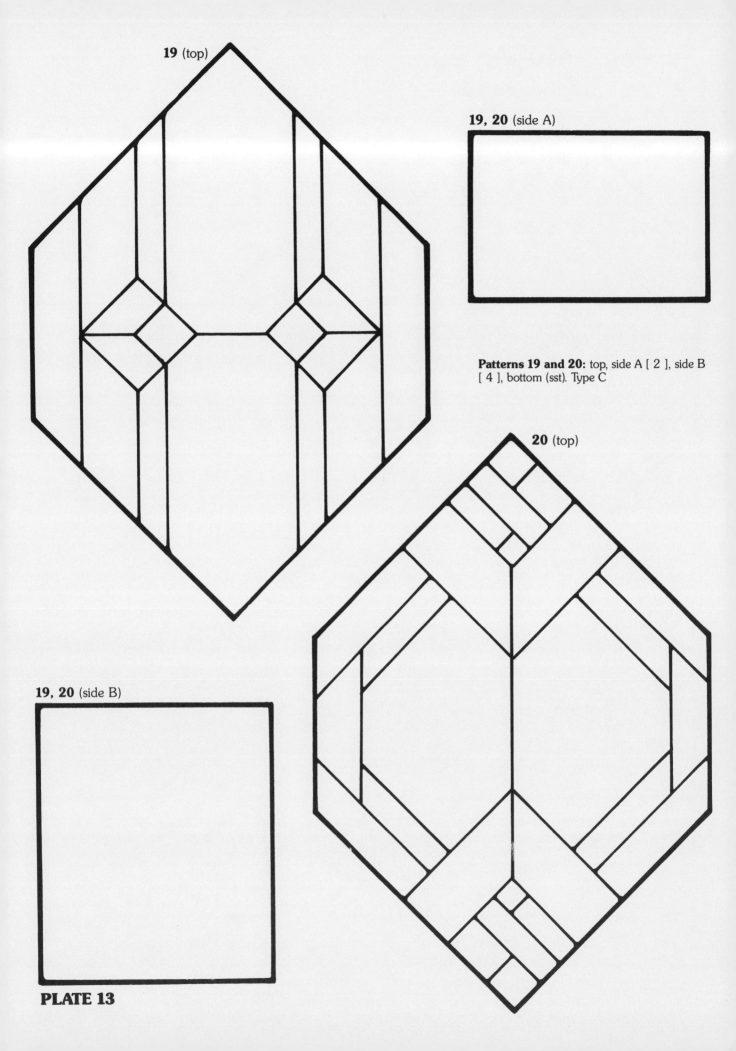

19 (top)

19, 20 (side A)

Patterns 19 and 20: top, side A [2], side B [4], bottom (sst). Type C

20 (top)

19, 20 (side B)

PLATE 13

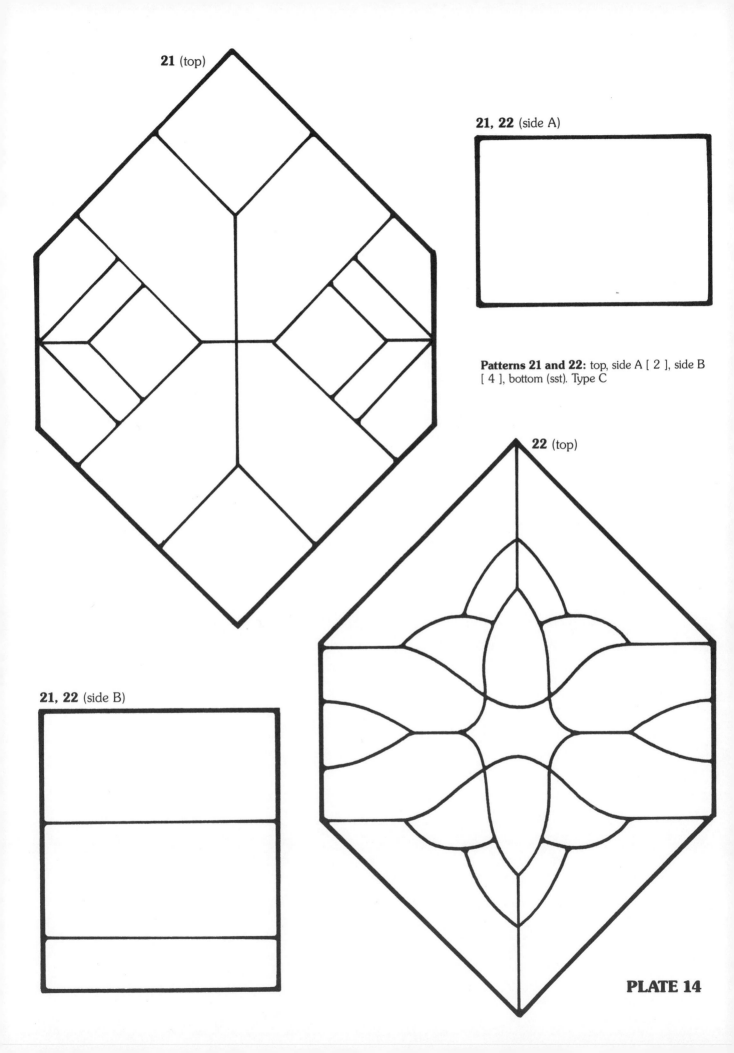

21 (top)

21, 22 (side A)

Patterns 21 and 22: top, side A [2], side B [4], bottom (sst). Type C

22 (top)

21, 22 (side B)

PLATE 14

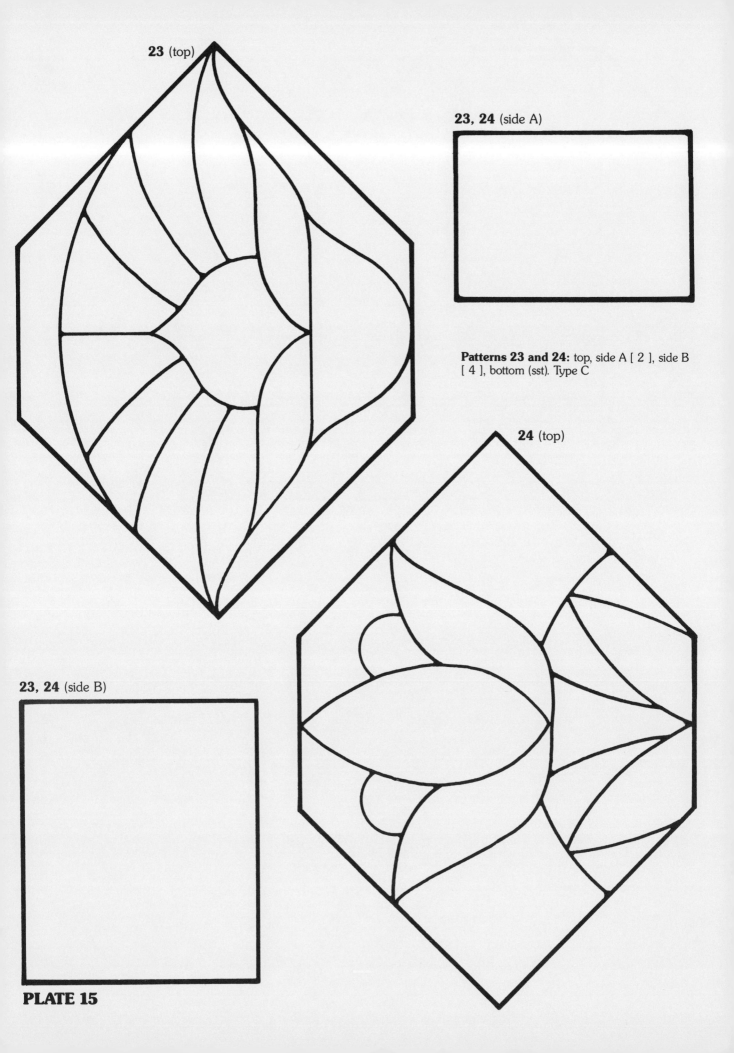

23 (top)

23, 24 (side A)

Patterns 23 and 24: top, side A [2], side B [4], bottom (sst). Type C

24 (top)

23, 24 (side B)

PLATE 15

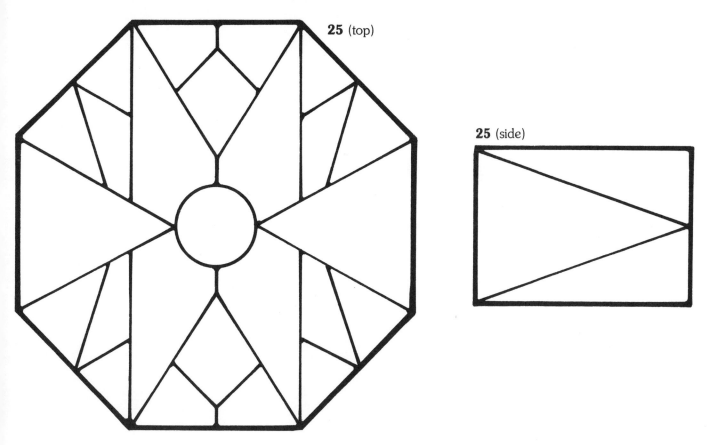

25 (top)

25 (side)

Patterns 25 and 26: top, side [8], bottom (sst). Type D

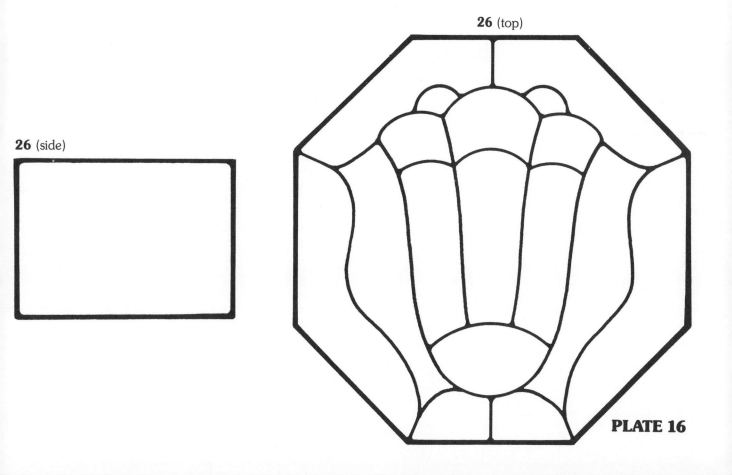

26 (top)

26 (side)

PLATE 16

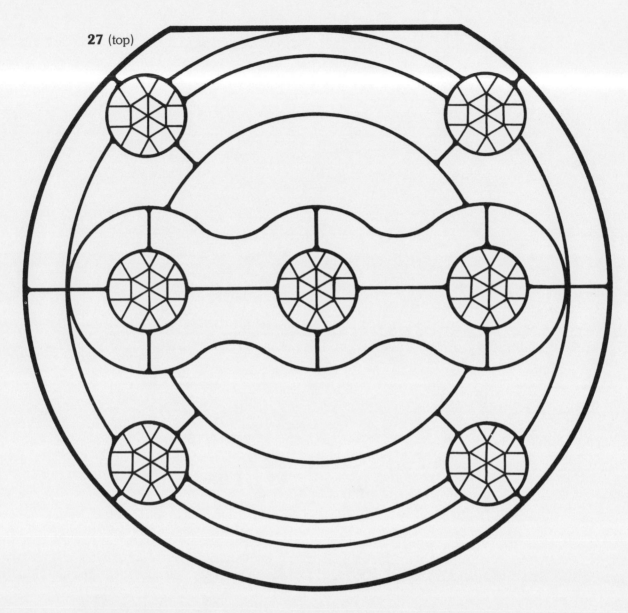

27 (top)

Pattern 27: top, back side, side templates [approximately 23—combined], bottom (sst). Type E

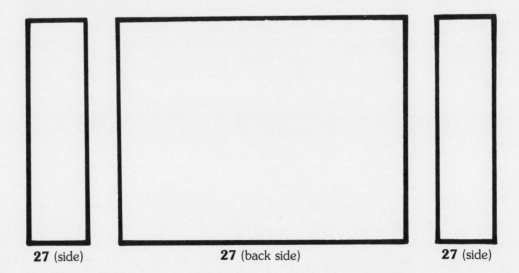

27 (side)   **27** (back side)   **27** (side)

PLATE 17

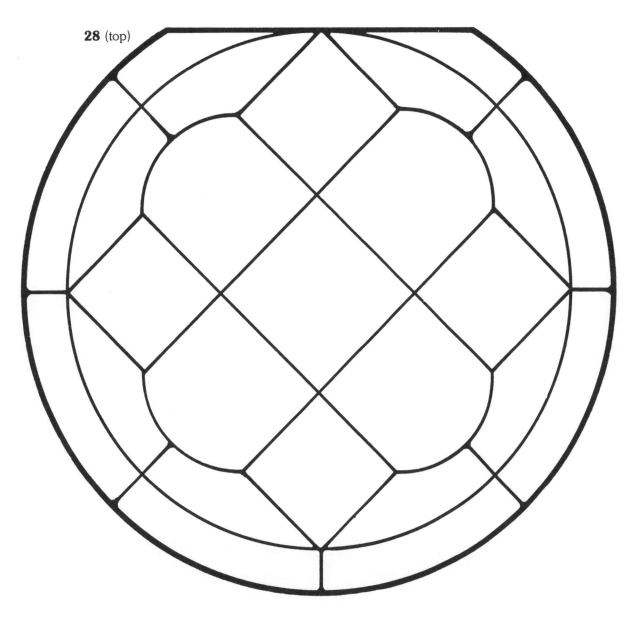

28 (top)

Pattern 28: top, back side, side templates [approximately 23—combined], bottom (sst). Type E

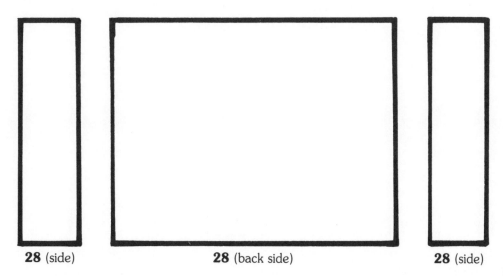

28 (side) **28** (back side) **28** (side)

PLATE 18

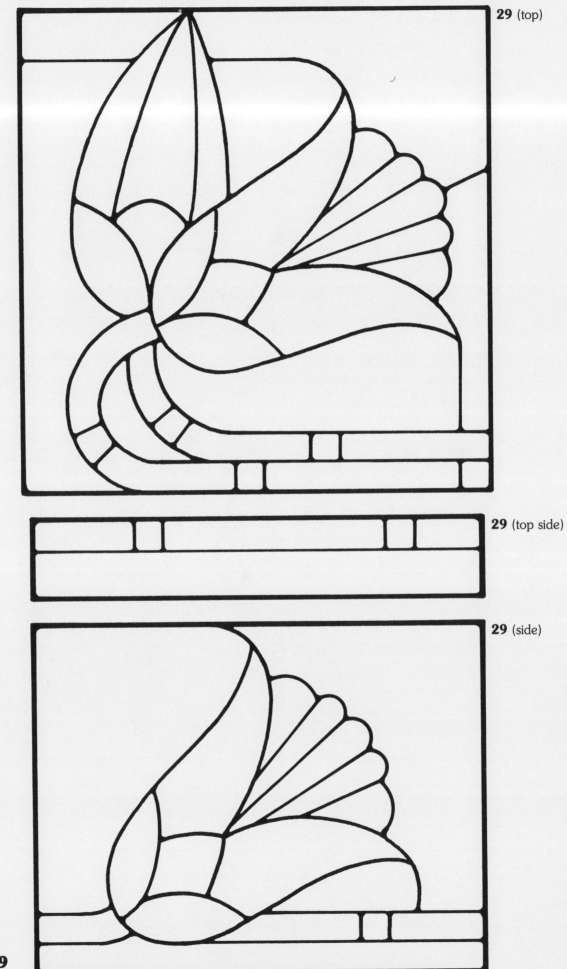

Pattern 29: top, top side [4], side [4], bottom (sst). Type F

29 (top)

29 (top side)

29 (side)

PLATE 19

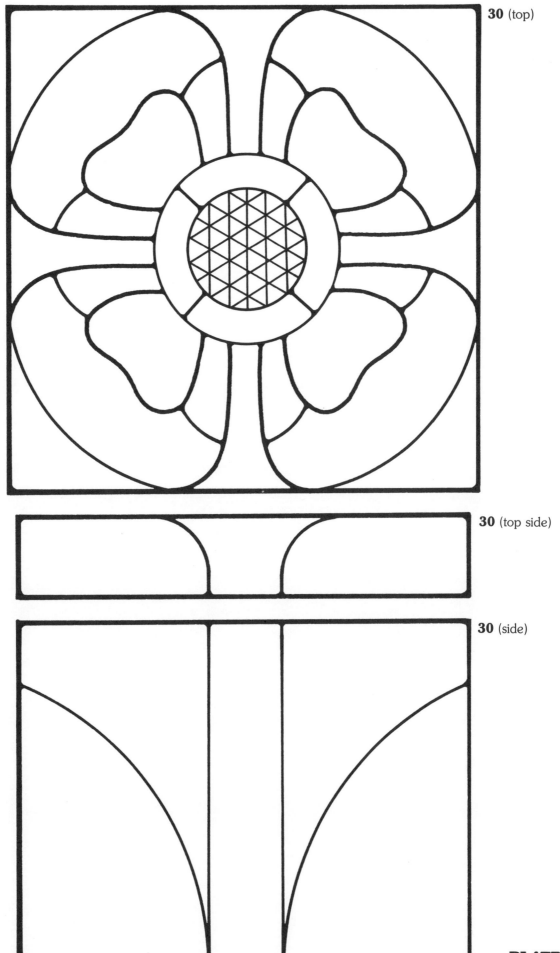

Pattern 30: top, top side [4], side [4], bottom (sst). Type F

30 (top)

30 (top side)

30 (side)

PLATE 20

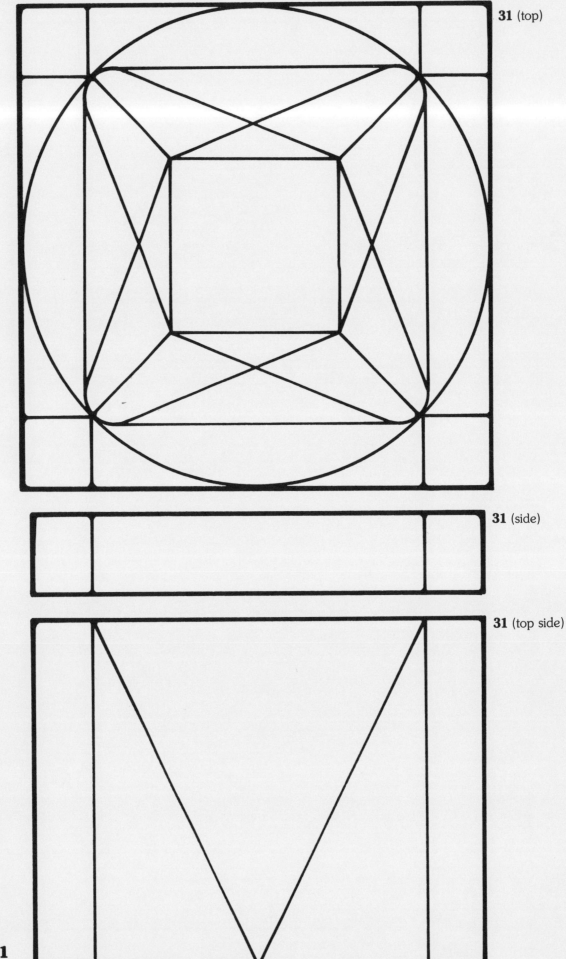

Pattern 31: top, top side [4], side [4], bottom (sst), Type F

31 (top)

31 (side)

31 (top side)

PLATE 21

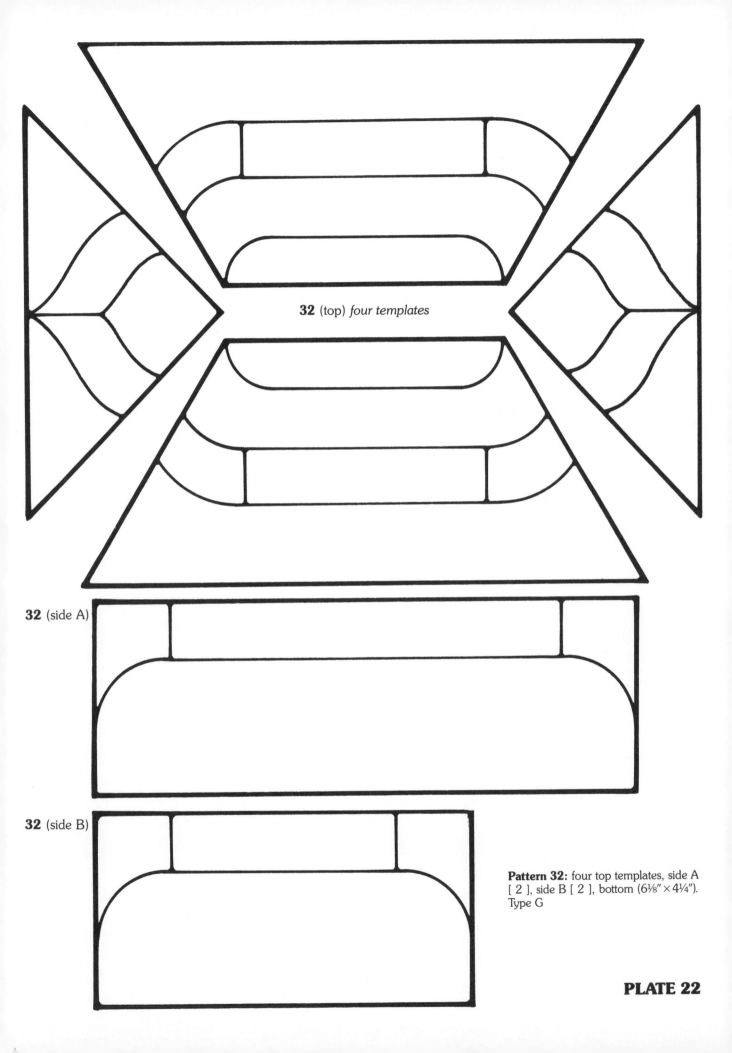

32 (top) *four templates*

32 (side A)

32 (side B)

Pattern 32: four top templates, side A
[2], side B [2], bottom (6⅛″ × 4¼″).
Type G

PLATE 22

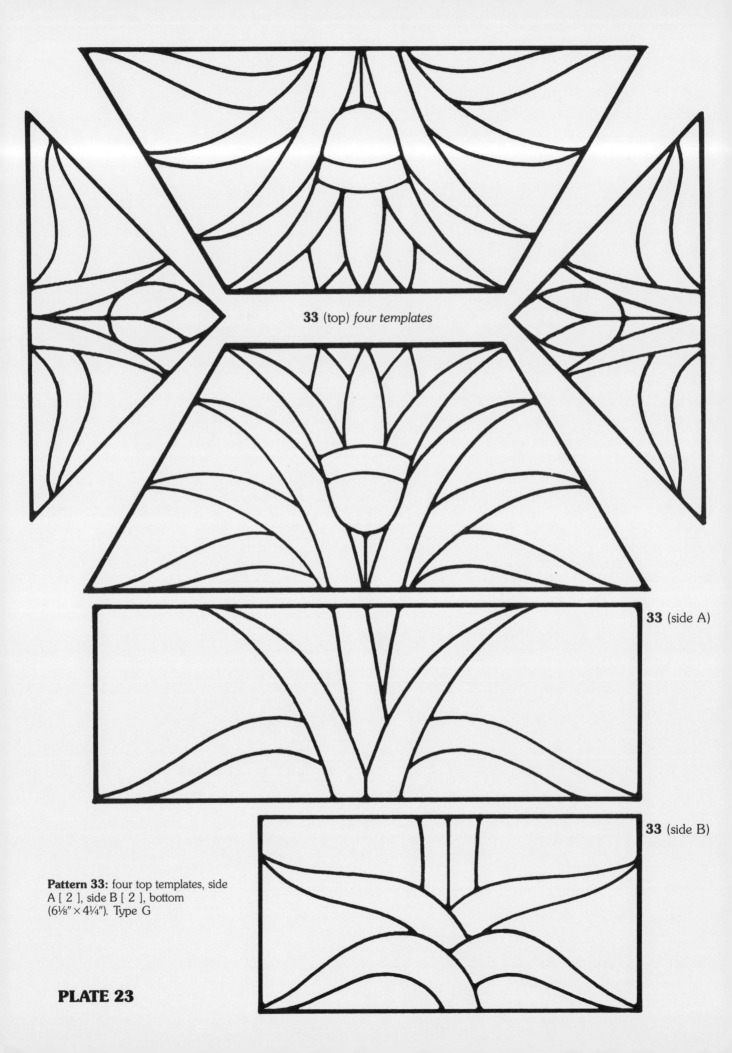

33 (top) *four templates*

33 (side A)

33 (side B)

Pattern 33: four top templates, side
A [2], side B [2], bottom
(6⅛″ × 4¼″). Type G

PLATE 23

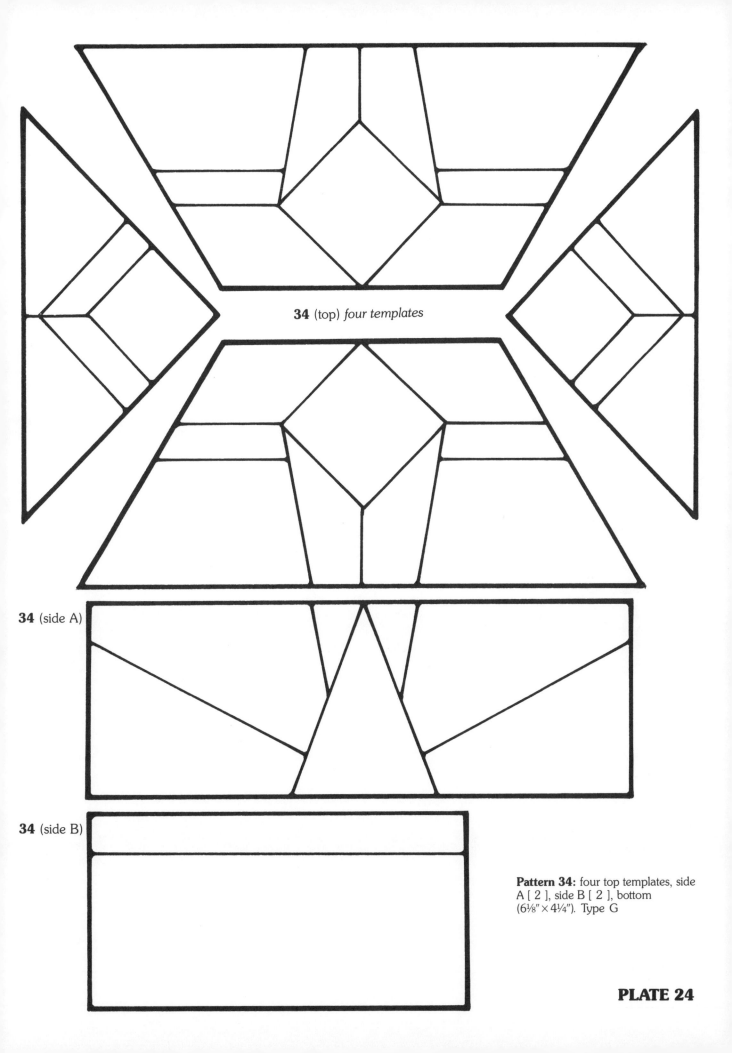

34 (top) *four templates*

34 (side A)

34 (side B)

Pattern 34: four top templates, side A [2], side B [2], bottom (6⅛″ × 4¼″). Type G

PLATE 24

35 (top) *in center*

35 (side A)

35 (top side A-1)

35 (top side B-1)

35 (top side A-2)

35 (top side B-2)

35 (side B)

Pattern 35: top, four top sides (A-1, A-2, B-1, B-2), side A [2], side B [2], bottom (7⅜″ × 4⅜″). Type H

PLATE 25

36 (top) *in center*

36 (side A)

36 (top side A)

36 (top side B)

36 (top side A)

36 (top side A)

36 (top side B)

Pattern 36: top, two top side A
templates, two top side B templates,
side A [2], side B [2], bottom
(7⅜″ × 4⅜″). Type H

36 (side B)

PLATE 26

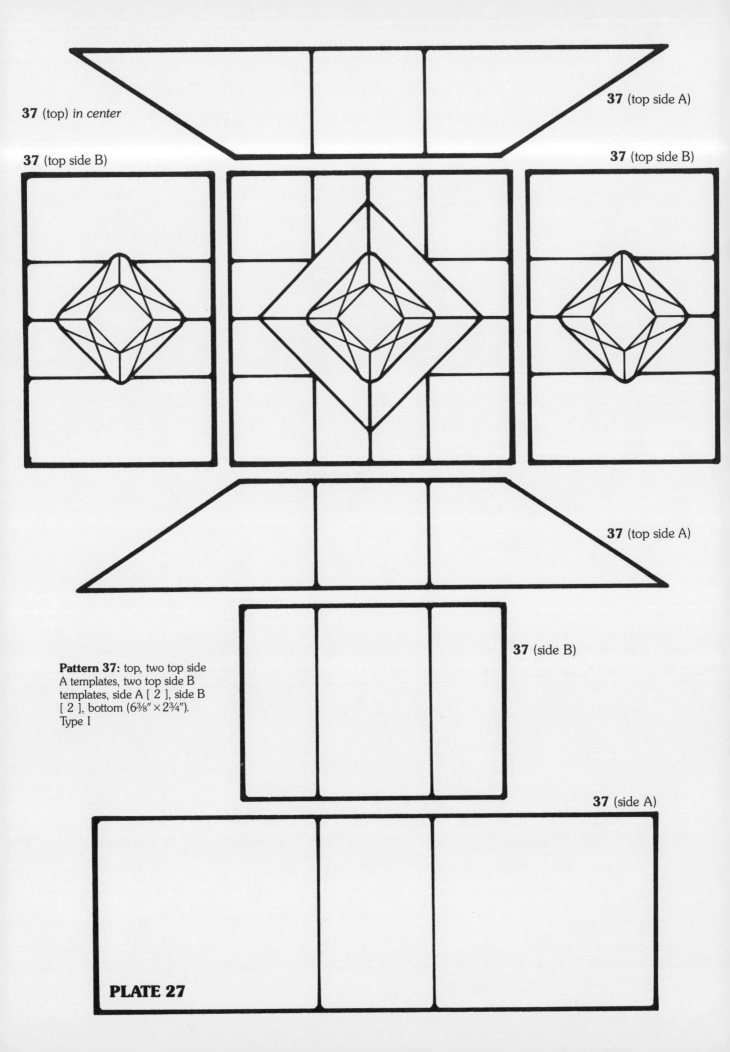

37 (top) *in center*

37 (top side A)

37 (top side B)

37 (top side B)

37 (top side A)

37 (side B)

Pattern 37: top, two top side A templates, two top side B templates, side A [2], side B [2], bottom (6⅜″ × 2¾″). Type I

37 (side A)

PLATE 27

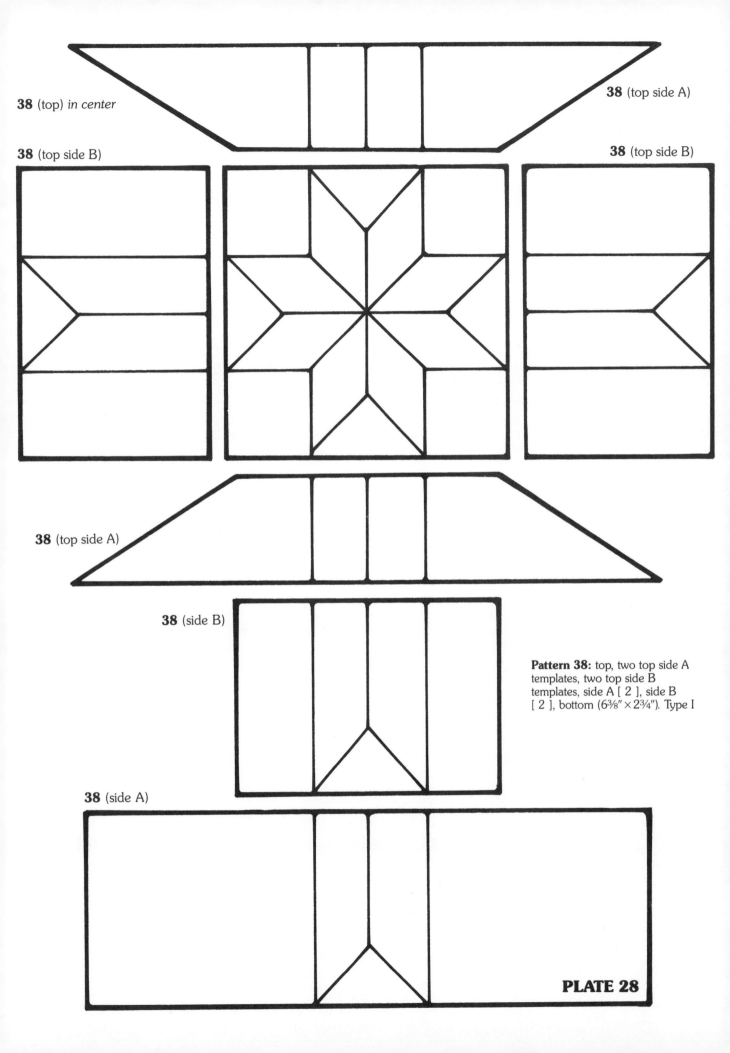

38 (top) *in center*

38 (top side A)

38 (top side B)

38 (top side B)

38 (top side A)

38 (side B)

Pattern 38: top, two top side A templates, two top side B templates, side A [2], side B [2], bottom (6⅜″ × 2¾″). Type I

38 (side A)

PLATE 28

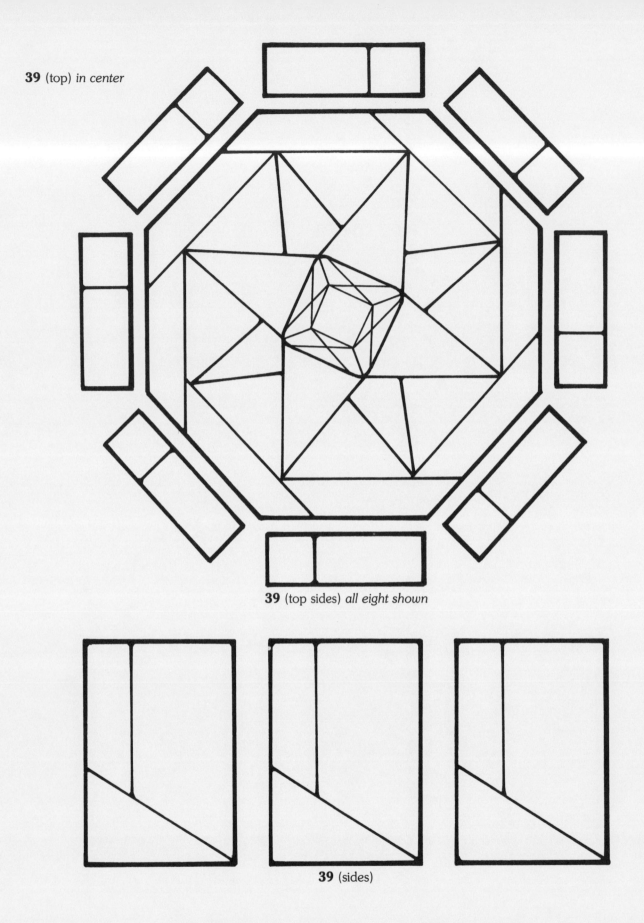

39 (top) *in center*

39 (top sides) *all eight shown*

39 (sides)

Pattern 39: top, eight top sides, sides [8—combined], bottom (sst). Type J

PLATE 29

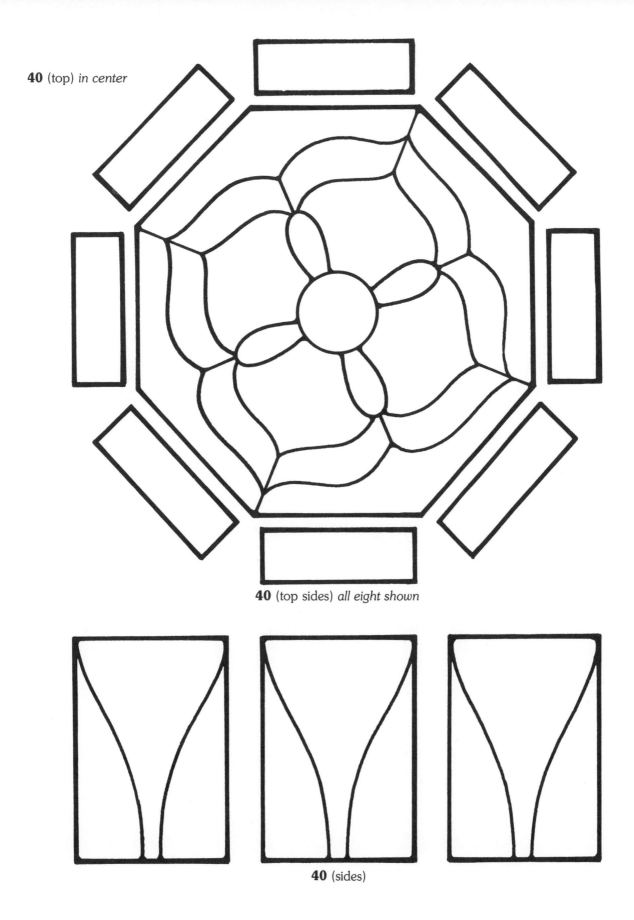

40 (top) *in center*

40 (top sides) *all eight shown*

40 (sides)

Pattern 40: top, eight top sides, sides [8—combined], bottom (sst). Type J

PLATE 30

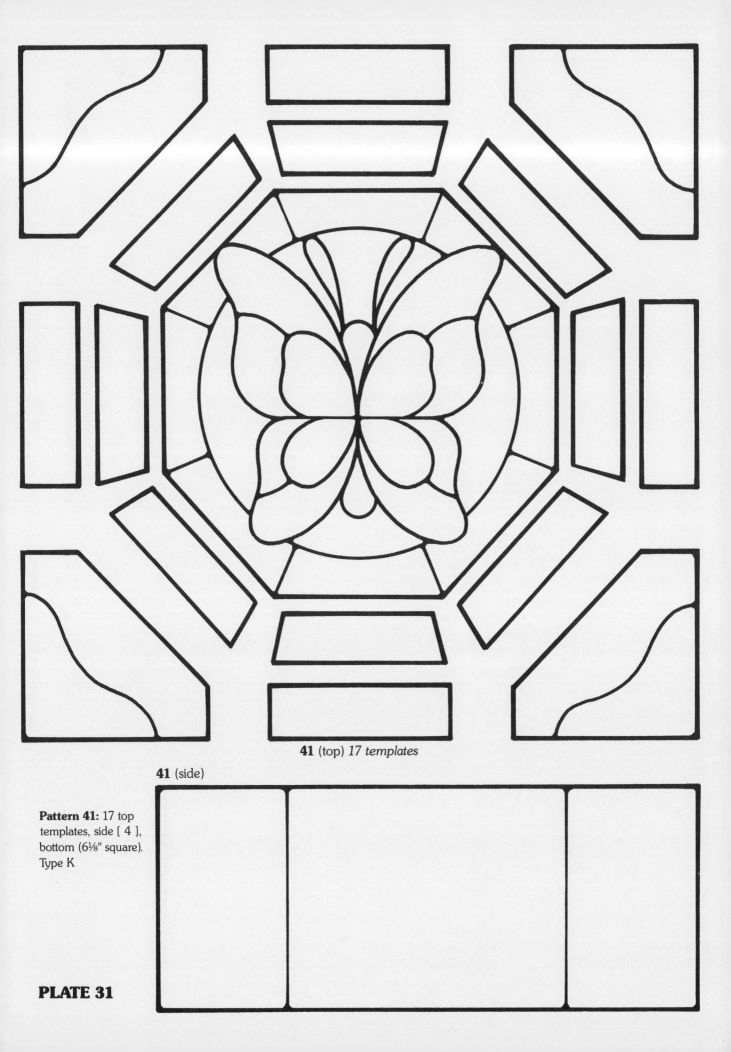

41 (top) *17 templates*

41 (side)

Pattern 41: 17 top
templates, side [4],
bottom (6⅛″ square).
Type K

PLATE 31

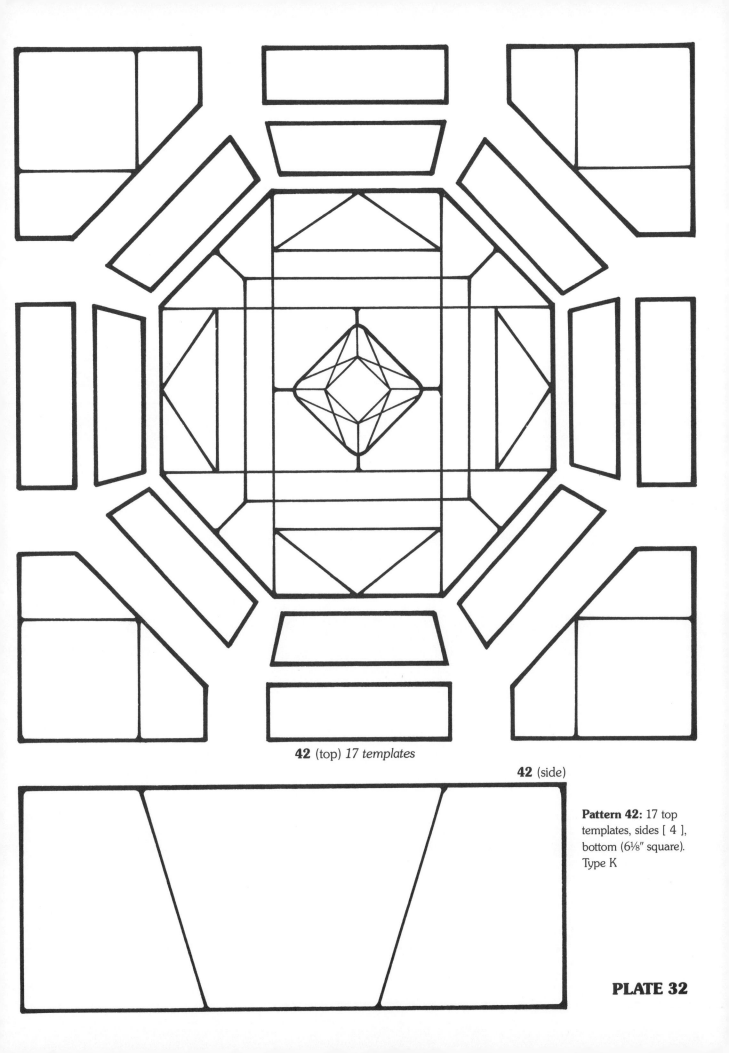

42 (top) *17 templates*

42 (side)

Pattern 42: 17 top
templates, sides [4],
bottom (6⅛″ square).
Type K

PLATE 32